There is an enhanced digital version of this book
with embedded videos available for download on
iTunes and Amazon.

Edited by Courtney Smith

#H2H Copyright ©2014 by Bryan Kramer

Substance Video Series Copyright ©2014 by PureMatter, Inc.

*Thank you to all the incredibly smart,
authentic and humble humans who helped make this
book a reality. You inspire me everyday.*

There is no B2B and B2C.

Human to Human: #H2H

Table of Contents

What is H2H?

Communication shouldn't be complicated. It should just be genuine and simple, with the humility and understanding that we're all multi-dimensional humans, every one of which has spent time in both the dark and delightful parts of life.

That's human to human.

Forward

Businesses do not have emotion. Products do not have emotion. Humans do.

Humans want to be a part of something bigger than themselves.

Humans want to be included. Humans want to feel something.

And humans make mistakes.

The concept of breaking down barriers in marketing is not a new one. For years, we've been saying at our agency that segmenting customers into business or consumer was an unnatural and unintuitive approach to marketing. My social friend, Mark Schaefer, wrote a great book called "The Tao of Twitter" in which he describes "P2P", or people to people.

But being in the business of communication here in Silicon Valley, and witnessing firsthand the explosion of new technologies from the likes of Google, eBay, Cisco, and countless startups, all maturing in the same space as some of the finest products in the world from Apple and Tesla, I saw the complexity around me. This complexity, combined with the rise of social and digital, had produced a pretty cold, anonymous ecosystem. We needed to bring back the human side of communication, in all its imperfection, empathy and simplicity.

I sense that others have hit the same threshold I have, in craving the real and authentic side of us all. This is what inspired H2H.

Chapter 1: The Unnatural Language of Business

Consumers are confused. With a whopping 93% of communication based on nonverbal body language, that leaves just 7% left to explain verbally what we really mean.

So why can't we make it simple for people to understand what we're selling, so they can more easily share their experiences and the value they felt with others? More importantly, why is it that what we're marketing most often does not align to actual consumer experiences?

I don't care what language you speak, who your brand is or what message you're trying to send, we all need to speak more human. Too often we complicate what we're trying to say. Ironically, as our world becomes more customer-owned and socially enabled, we continue to see complicated, redundant, over-technical, and over-thought mass messages getting pushed out – and lost – in the ether. Is it really getting harder to stand out, with so much data and information out there… or is the answer just to clearly say what you mean, in understandable human words?

The fact is that the lines are so far blurred now between the "B2C" (Business to Consumer) and "B2B" (Business to Business) marketing segments that it's hard to differentiate between the two anymore. Why do business marketers think they need to speak differently to their audience? I can't tell you how many meetings I've been in where acronyms are used so often that my brain ends up spending so much time trying to decipher what they mean instead of focusing on the actual thoughts trying to be conveyed. Acronyms have their place, but not when they replace communicating information to someone else who might not understand your world full of capital letters. We all need to think like the consumers we are, putting ourselves in the mind set of the buyer instead of trying to speak such an intensely sophisticated language full of acronyms and big words, in order to sound smarter.

The same is true for social. We have new acronyms like LOL. OMG. TY. BRB. New words like Selfie, Hashtag, Wiki and Tag. These terms have their own new "assigned" meaning, and have helped us gain a new way of conversing with each other. In quick statements, letters, sometimes pictures and memes, we're learning to speak a new language. Full proper sentences are becoming a thing of the past when it comes to short engagement, like on Twitter and text, because technology demands a way for us to communicate in a new way. Is it really making us more efficient? Or maybe it's evidence of our need as humans to continually evolve? It could be that each "network" has it's own nuance of sharing – whether a social network, or the human network – colliding worlds in our short and long-form conversations and requiring us to relearn how to share with each other in a greater context than ever before.

Jill Brewbaker Rowley IRL
January 12 at 5:02pm · Like · 👍 3

Rich Greenwood WTF I totally overuse that term too! OMG
January 12 at 5:03pm · Like · 👍 1

Mike Ellsworth TL;DR
January 12 at 5:08pm · Like · 👍 2

David Fiss FYI
January 12 at 5:13pm · Like · 👍 1

Dave Cox ILYSM & SHMILY
January 12 at 5:17pm · Like · 👍 2

Sue Lancaster WTG Bryan!
January 12 at 5:19pm · Like · 👍 1

Lou De La Rosa BTW (by the way). I rarely use others as I generally detest acronyms.
January 12 at 5:23pm · Like · 👍 2

Mark Waxman URUTMA (you are using too many acronyms)
January 12 at 5:27pm · Like · 👍 1

Lori Ruff BRB is my favorite as it allows me to quickly warn a chat buddy I'll be gone a couple mins (usually cause I gotta go pee!) but I use OMG (Oh my gosh) or OMGosh most often.
January 12 at 5:33pm · Like · 👍 2

Paul Bradshaw LMK, WTF, USA.
January 12 at 5:33pm · Like · 👍 1

Adam Helweh ROFLCOPTER
January 12 at 5:34pm · Like · 👍 4

Mike Ellsworth Greg, I was thinking Family Medical Leave . . .
January 12 at 5:35pm · Like · 👍 1

T Scott Clendaniel YMMV Your mileage may vary.
January 12 at 5:35pm · Like · 👍 2

Mike Ellsworth I like FWIW because it expresses humility. Possibly why it's not seen that much anymore . . .
January 12 at 5:36pm · Like · 👍 1

My Facebook experiment on people's favorite social acronyms. I got some good ones!

Context: The Killer of Confusion

Words are just words. Stories are just stories. But with context, concepts come alive. According to Dictionary.com, Context is "the circumstances that form the setting for an event, statement or idea, in terms by which it can be fully understood." In other words, it's not just about the message, it's almost more importantly about everything happening *around* the message that gives it meaning. Humans understand and process information in context. For marketers, this means understanding where your audience will consume the information they receive (Mobile? Tablet? Laptop?), as well as the mindset they're likely in when they receive it, so they'll pay attention. For instance, do you know what their top business pains are? And how is what you're offering a "pain killer" to these business pains?

In social, content is important, but *context* is HUGE. If your content is not in the right context for both your specific social media platform and for the audience you want to engage, it's a social gunshot – throwing a bunch of words in the air and hoping that, somehow, somewhere, they land on a few people in a way that makes sense and captures their attention.

Providing the right context in social sharing is an art form. The words that you Tweet, post or write are planting the seed for the experience. When your audience takes your message, and relates it to their life in a new way, that's when the experience blossoms. The Socialsphere is a place where we present our thoughts and ideas to the world, where the challenge lies in making those thoughts and ideas connect with our audience.

What do I share and how do I share it? What will resonate? Will I lose likes or followers? It's tough, right? I do believe this—the more authentic you are, the more you will get out of your share. But you have to be mindful of context when you share, always.

Here are four ways I try to do that before deploying any social effort.

The Four Rules of Social Context

1. **Think it through.** (or, as Courtney Smith, our company co-founder and Executive Creative Director likes to say, "TITS: Think it Through, SERIOUSLY.") In order to do this, whether it's a blog or a Tweet, you need to visualize how what you share will play out, and whether it meets your objectives. Everything you share should be true to your brand – personal and company – to support your goals and have a purpose. This is where many social sharers have witnessed their demise, in Tweeting something snarky or inappropriate, either from their own handle or a corporate handle by mistake. I hear almost weekly of someone getting fired for tweeting something inappropriate. This can be avoided by simply thinking it through (seriously.)

2. **Skip to the last page first.** In other words, know the end as well as the beginning when you plan your strategy. This is the difference between creating something complicated and complex. Complex systems work because there's a beginning and an end point, with the trick being figuring out the best way to connect the two points. Complicated systems have one or the other.

You don't want to lead your audience down a path that just starts meandering aimlessly—they'll likely not stick with you. You have to know what direction you're heading in your message. Always. P.S. Don't deviate. And if you do, redefine the end.

3. **Slow down.** How many times have you Tweeted, posted, blogged, updated—just pushed a message out there so you can check it off your list? We live in a fast-paced world where if you move too quickly, you forget to put effort into the moment that could potentially be a creative and thoughtful experience. Courtney always says that when she gets behind a computer, somehow time tends to slow down and she enters a time warp. I don't know how she does it, but she always comes out with the most incredible creative product and has learned to harness time and not rush the process. When you give yourself time to reflect on what you're creating, you'll enter your audience's world—and then you'll deliver a message that will resonate.

4. **Get out of your head.** It's time to break out of that old habit of thinking everyone knows what's rattling around in your brain and look at what you're sharing from an outsider's point of view. Ask someone on your staff, a friend, a colleague, "does this make sense to you?" before you post something. Get objective opinions. Be you, yes—be true to your thoughts and opinions. But express them in a way that people "get" you. Sometimes that means sharing your own context along with your message.

Key takeaway: It's not just about what you share, it's about how you share it and thinking through how people will likely receive it. Content provides a message, but context creates the experience and the connection that you're trying to achieve. Social media is challenging that way because context varies, but if you share authentically and know your audience, you'll create more meaningful social experiences that people want to be a part of.

Chapter 2: How to Speak Human: Tapping into our Needs and Senses

Humans are social creatures; this is something we all know and understand. I had the pleasure of interviewing Scott Hebner, VP of Social Business at IBM, and friend Kare Anderson, author, speaker, columnist and coach, about how human behavior fits into the context of social marketing. Given that humans consume socially, I wondered where social marketing is headed as it continues to mature. Both Scott and Kare explained in their own ways that the future of social marketing involves "human sensory building", and how it will become necessary to intertwine this approach into the marketing experience at each stage of the customer lifecycle. When we are able to weave directly relatable human experiences into social situations, it changes how we share and consume information forever.

What does Human Sensory Building mean?

Human Sensory Building means connecting marketing to our most basic human sensory system. The more you can map what you're communicating to these senses, the deeper and more meaningful your connections will be.

Here are a few examples:

Sight: For some reason, design is often overlooked in product design, to its own demise. Think your IT or engineering audience doesn't care about great-looking marketing? Think again. Design matters; as humans, we naturally appreciate nice looking things.

Touch: In both senses of the word, the physical act of touching something, and the emotional touching of others. Feel what you're saying. If you connect with what's being said, others will too. Think through the experience you want your users to have in the context of how they're consuming it. Make it tactile. Make it a game. Make it interactive. Whatever your choices, make it meaningful for them. You'll know when it's meaningful for you.

Listening: This is the mother of all skills when it comes to successful conversations. You'd think being good at this is fundamental, but it's not. Actively listening, in the context of social media, means monitoring social conversations, and joining in. By joining into new conversations, you'll quickly see new opportunities to engage, answer questions, solve a problem, whatever the other person is sharing about your brand. And when they're heard, and helped, they become interested and endeared – at the very least, neutralized – and are more inclined to share and purchase from you.

Brands are presented with "shining moment" opportunities every day to create positive interactions with their customers, both happy and not. Have you ever shared your comments with another human over email and they simply never responded? Most brands I come into contact with are afraid to reply back, because if they reply back to one, they think they have to reply back to everyone. Not true! There are unique conversations that do not deserve to be dismissed. When a consumer builds up the courage to tweet a brand and broadcast their unique experience (as a thank you or negative feedback), the worst thing they could receive is radio silence. Just like in real life, when people want to talk and it falls on deaf ears, the perception is "they don't care." That moment when a brand could have taken someone from a fan to raving but misses the opportunity is what I call a "wrecking ball" to the brand.

"86% of online consumer feedback is missed by brands."
~ Social Media Examiner

You can spare your brand from the wrecking ball by really listening. Actively listening in social allows you to hear those golden nuggets of feedback, criticism and praise that empower brands to perform random acts of social marketing kindness that makes social media relatable to our offline lives.

I'm talking about that moment when someone gets their hotel room upgraded, simply because a social brand ambassador saw a Tweet about them not having a good experience. These little moments of random social kindness become utterly unforgettable, starting off as small gestures but growing into shareable stories because someone reached out with unexpected care.

Sometimes large brands can really get themselves in trouble if they choose to publicly take part in universally known events without a structured social program in place, such as remembering the 9/11 tragedies. Here's a recent example pulled from The Huffington Post, in where someone at an independent Marriott franchise, whom we can assume had good intentions, decided to offer free coffee and mini-muffins for a WHOLE HALF HOUR during breakfast to honor those lost in 9/11. A guest saw this, snapped a picture, and Tweeted it out. The Tweet went viral as people shared it in disbelief – 5,365 times to be exact – and because Marriott wasn't socially listening (or seemed not to be due to their lack of immediate response), it took their corporate office 2 days to respond with an apology. Via email. To the Huffington Post.

What pic.twitter.com/L35ytAtCWP
8:52 AM - 11 Sep 2013

While the hotel was making a sympathetic gesture to its guests in remembrance of 9/11, we apologize and understand why some people may have misunderstood the intent of the offer.

Marriott's emailed response to Huffington Post **2 days later**

5,366 RETWEETS 2,808 FAVORITES

Image Source: Huffington Post

By Marriott not actively listening and taking part in the social conversation, you can imagine the negative sentiment they had to battle and spend time, money and resources to mitigate the incident.

Now, I love Marriott, don't get me wrong – but this is a great example that even brands we love are in the constant cross hairs of an incident if they're not actively listening across social.

Key takeaway: Consumers today have the highest of expectations. But it doesn't take massive software, complicated strategies or tons of people to meet them. Just be human and meet them where they are; listen, respond, have a conversation, and you'll create customers for life.

Understanding the Six Basic Human Needs

Over the years, I've adopted the "Six Basic Human Needs" that Tony Robbins uses as a foundation in his teaching. They have given me a powerful set of tools to understand the common human psychological connections we all share; Tapping into this core set of values in your marketing initiatives will give your efforts a real boost of human energy that will activate your audience into action.

Connection/Love. People need to feel connected – to themselves, their families, their community, their country, their planet, their universe – and for brands, it goes without saying that if you can't connect with your audience, you need to identify the problem and approach it differently. This is why communities exist; people need to connect and feel affirmed by other like-minded people.

Significance. We all need to be acknowledged for a job well done. We need to own our own hilltop somewhere. We need to be the star of our own movie. This is why awards exist.

Variety/Uncertainty. Everybody loves an adventure. A ride. The unpredictable. As humans, we need things to be different so we don't die of boredom.

Certainty. We all want to know what's going to happen. We need things to be the same so there are no surprises. This is why schedules and rhythm are fundamentally important to humanity; certain things make us feel safe and protected.

Growth. I constantly marvel at people who proclaim that they're happy with themselves exactly as they are right now. Every human being has a need to grow – mentally, cerebrally, psychologically, ethically – in other words, we were built to never stop learning.

Contribution. Everyone needs to feel like what they're doing is making a difference. In work, we need to feel like an important contributor to the success of the company. We donate our time to help others in need. In any case, we all need to feel like what we're doing matters, and matters for a reason that is greater than ourselves.

Key takeaway: Being mindful of these needs when you're crafting a social campaign, or just socially interacting with others, can make the difference between creating something that motivates others to act, or just falls flat.

Celebrating our "Focker" Moments

No, that's not a typo; it's a reference to my favorite movie character Gaylord Focker, as played by Ben Stiller in the "Meet the Parents" movie trilogy. What I love about Gaylord Focker is he's a kind-hearted, smart and humble guy who happens, through a series of misguided good intentions, to make mistake after mistake. He's lovable, laughable, and in my opinion, a fantastic example of what it's like to be truly human. I have had many "Focker" moments in my own life, all of which have become part of my own storytelling lore that makes me feel connected to my true and authentic self. Who hasn't sat through a meeting with their fly down? Who hasn't accidentally walked into the wrong public bathroom and realized it just a little too late? Yes, I am talking to you. You know who you are. Embracing our own "Focker" moments in life helps us become better storytellers and social sharers. Being able to laugh at yourself is one of the most endearing traits we as humans have.

"When you're a really great marketer, your goal is to be one step ahead of the market. You need the ability to peer around corners. That means you have to be willing to be wrong."

~ Jonathan Becher, CMO, SAP

Of course, it's in our nature to strive for success, but as humans, we can't help but make mistakes. Charlene Li, author of "Groundswell" and co-founder of The Altimeter Group, in a recent Substance interview (PureMatter's Luminary Video series) we did together, explains that she is a huge believer in failure. But why are so many people afraid to take this chance? "People want to live in the veneer of success; look at Facebook, and the things people post. Everything is great and it's rare for people to appropriately post about their struggle. When you live by "Fail often and fail smart", meaning ask for forgiveness in trying new things, and if you fail in 1 out 3, learn from what didn't work and move on from there," says Li.

Learning is a fundamental human trait. As marketers, part of our role is to not only help others become successful through teaching and learning, but to go through the process with eyes wide open to keep making things better in our own work.

Many of you may know that my friend DJ Waldow and I recently conducted a 90-day experiment to see if we could use only social media to build a real relationship with Ellen DeGeneres (90DaysToEllen.com) by landing lunch with her in an effort to raise money for Feeding America®. The experiment, by the numbers, was a huge success; generating almost 70 million impressions across social channels, almost 100 videos created by an ever-growing community of fans, dozens of memes and over $1500 raised for Feeding America – all for a budget of less than dinner for two. By the outcome, it was a huge failure – not only did we not land lunch with

Ellen, but she never even acknowledged the effort. The part
we never could have predicted is that we actually proved our
hypothesis to be true, just in an unexpected way; social can
build relationships and raise money for Feeding America; just
not with Ellen.

We forged relationships with hundreds of people around the
globe who got behind the effort to help make this happen.
Their participation directly helped us gained momentum
because we engaged in catch and release conversation, and
implemented their ideas. The campaign itself was a 2-way
conversation with everyone involved – except for Ellen.

Now, not to sound like sour grapes, because I still really like
Ellen; But the fact that her team, and she, weren't actively
listening, put her brand at risk for the wrecking ball. Here's
a recent Facebook post from one of my friends, a fellow
marketer, who publicly voices her feelings about watching the
new season of the Ellen Degeneres show.

I appreciate her understanding that the spirit of the
campaign was not negative. But the fact that we received no
acknowledgement from the Ellen camp made an impression
nonetheless.

I can guarantee that if Ellen – even someone on her team eight levels below Ellen herself – had just responded with a simple "no thank you", the sentiment for her would have been much different.

Keep in mind, our campaign was miniscule compared to what really big brands could pull off. But more and more, things like this are happening every day, on social and across the web.

Chapter 3: Humans Just Want to be Heard

Customers, as humans, are fickle and are so empowered today that they expect extraordinary, over-the-top experiences that rock their world. Nothing less will do. Gone are the days where feedback was kept quiet and experiences were collected around a review form. Today, your customer's comments are transparent to your competitors, making it easier for them to publicly see your pain points. Comparisons are easier to make and product switching happens faster than ever. Customers are ready to move on unless they have one thing – an undying relationship with a person or people at your brand who made them feel uniquely special.

Have you ever done a search for the hashtag #fail on Twitter? I ran a social listening report and analyzed, over a 30 day period, the term "#fail" versus a much more positive term,

"#thankyou". As you can probably guess, #fail appeared 578,532 times – or 68% – versus just 264,985 – or 32% – for #thankyou. Clearly, complaining on social is much easier than complimenting. Customers legitimately have higher expectations for brands than ever before, and have a very loud and anonymous voice through social.

> "When you do for others without expecting anything in return, people rally around you and support you in ways you could never expect."
>
> ~ Ted Rubin

Jay Baer, author of "YouTility: Why Smart Marketing is About Help, Not Hype", has a great philosophy that I love. He explains, "If you're wondering how to make your products seem more exciting online, you're asking the wrong question. You're not competing for attention only against other similar products. You're competing against your customers' friends and family and viral videos and cute puppies. To win attention these days you must ask a different question: "How can we help?" He explains, in very wise words, that " If you sell something, you make a customer today, but if you genuinely help someone, you create a customer for life." Amen, brother.

You might think that helping others comes naturally to the human race, but for most people, it doesn't. Yet on the social

give give give give give give give give give give give give give give give give give give give give get.

#H2H @bryankramer

web, it's the single most effective form of earning trust and gaining influence.

And at any given moment, someone is trying to earn something from someone. Whether it's trust, loyalty respect, even love, it's the intangibles that people desire but can never buy. As humans, we want to be heard, and know that someone out there is listening.

As humans, we are also built to receive, give and disseminate information. The gravitational pull we're in is advancing our technology into unfathomable speeds, creating conversations of both excitement and disdain for humans to keep up. And yet, we continue to evolve faster than ever.

And in the eyes of a brand, there is no better way to create loyal customers than to show them that they matter.

But how do you scale to make everyone feel like they matter?

If the Internet were a city, it would be the most awake city in the world, generating more conversations than 24/7 places like New Orleans and Vegas combined. There are over 1.5 billion tweets generated every 2 days and over 30 billion pieces of content shared each month on Facebook (Kiss Metrics). So how do you scale listening and interacting as a large brand? Becoming a Social Business takes time but it's where business is headed, and those who embrace this paradigm shift will win.

Empowering people to be social within big brands is a pretty scary prospect for most executives. Traditionally, a CMO (Chief Marketing Officer) would carefully craft its brand position and aesthetic, architect a brand hierarchy and release it into the wild as a one-way conversation. But today, as a social business, the role of a CMO is very different; the necessary skills and qualifications are shifting with the shift toward social business.

I recently got to interview Jonathan Becher, CMO of SAP, on the topic of Social Business. He believes that Marketing has always been the glue in a company. But future marketing and future PR are two sides of the same coin. "Social forces companies to break down internal barriers. If you think of social as a shouting platform, then you can go onto your platforms and send it out and you're done," said Becher.

He explains that social is an interaction platform that requires the routing of conversations to the right people to get the right answers. The person asking the question doesn't care what department the social employee is in; they just want their question answered. "Business needs to work from the inside out and ask themselves 'what do our customers want?'"

But true social businesses are few and far between today, only because the complexities and data is so overwhelming. Becoming a business that perpetuates creative problem solving powered by social today means you first have to listen in order to keep up. It's important that businesses use social to co-create ideas and innovation. We still need leadership and vision, but the power of one top-down voice is gone.

Are most companies ready and enabled to approach social in this way? Short answer: No. I believe they are divided into three very distinct categories, driven by various levels of fear.

1) Fear of not being on social media so they jump right in without a plan.

2) Fear of saying the wrong thing so they don't take part at all.

3) Fear of what engaging means for their company so they use social as a one-way conversation.

The question for brands is this: Would you rather be a part of the conversation, or let others make assumptions about how you feel and what you think?

A Simplified Approach to Social Business

Find yourself a social savvy team to engage with your social communities.

Develop processes, such as social governance and response models to set boundaries specific to your brand values.

Find and test social and measurement tools that serve your business goals best.

When you integrate social into your people, processes and technology, you humanize your business at every touch point.

The worst thing you can do is nothing. And not every brand gets it right.

Here's an example of the wrecking ball in action, this one from Todd Wilms, Head of Social Business for SAP, as told by him in a webinar we did together.

FedEx Case Study: Making it Right When You Get it Wrong

At some point in their life cycle, virtually every company will be faced with a PR crisis of some kind. Social media has really amplified corporate mistakes and it's not uncommon for missteps to be broadcast within hours or even minutes of their occurrence. In these situations, the only option is to be reactive and to go on the defensive in order to mitigate brand damage. Being in a reactive position is certainly not ideal but within that space there are a lot of choices to be made about what damage control looks like. Thanks to the actions of one less than stellar employee, FedEx has provided a great case study in reactive crisis management.

People around the world – now over 9 million of them - watched a video taken last Christmas from a home security camera of a FedEx delivery man take a computer monitor and, instead of ringing the bell, just throwing it over the wall. The important thing to note is that people watching this video were likely not really looking at this individual but at what is prominently displayed in the background; the FedEx truck. From a brand management standpoint, what was upsetting was that the delivery man didn't even ring the bell; had he done so he would have found that the package recipient was home. He didn't do anything but pick up the packaged TV and throw it over the wall with complete disregard for the experience he was creating for the customer, all with FedEx prominently displayed in the background.

FedEx could have responded to this issue in a number of ways to try to shift the blame. For example, they could have accused UPS of playing a prank by dressing up as one of their employees in a FedEx uniform as a ploy to damage the company's reputation during its peak season. Instead, they took the high road and owned up to the problem. Rather than trot out a slick PR professional or a smooth, fast-talking marketing person, they had a spokesman from their operations department address the issue. He didn't shift blame and he didn't tap dance. He was humble, genuinely nervous and clearly not someone who was used to being on camera. FedEx didn't just admit there was a problem; they outlined how the problem was being fixed internally. Next, they did more than own the mistake, they demonstrated they had learned from the instance and were taking steps so that it would never be an issue again. Then, they told people where to go for help. People vote for brands with their wallets: When the computer monitor toss video went viral, FedEx stock took a sharp dive. When their sincere apology was made, it rose slightly but took over 30 days of no media coverage about the incident to fully recover.

I wonder, if FedEx had responded sooner through their social channels, would they have had the same outcome? They do get points for responding in an authentic way and owning up to their mistake, which humanized their brand to me.

Actively listening and responding gives brands the greatest opportunity to grow your tribe of loyal fans. If you're consistent, authentic and honest, they will stick with you through the bad times, and will always be eager to help and share. As a business, this means revenue for you. But more importantly, it means you care about your customers, your employees, your company, and your product. It means taking pride in serving others in the right way. Isn't that why we're all here anyway?

Chapter 4: The Human Need to be Disruptive

According to Charlene Li, disruption is a way of life. "We constantly talk about innovation, but today it's table stakes. Brands need to constantly think about how they would destroy their business, and how it would make their company better," Li explains. "Small business can innovate more quickly, but large companies have scale. We often underestimate the power of scale; they are suited to find the fast leaders and acquire them, then try to do it better. But what's the relationship between Social Business, disruption, and innovation? Social causes much of this disruption within businesses. Executives aren't sure how to handle this change in relationship with their internal teams and customers. It's a shift in the power relationship, which is why people fear it and are drawn to it at the same time."

Disruption isn't only necessary internally with employees. How a brand communicates to its external audience is also "table stakes" in today's noisy and cluttered world. As marketers, we strive to create highly personal interactions as much as possible, to develop strong bonds with our buyers. On the other hand, we rely on the "crowd" to shift power in the form of share of voice, share of market, and share of wallet – and sometimes, crowds can be downright unruly.

How do you humanize a crowd?

There is no shortage of people in social. But just like in life, if you run with the wrong crowd, what you have to offer will never be maximized or heard.

Social identity theory states that the self is a complex system made up primarily of the concept of membership or non-membership in various social groups. (*Source: Wikipedia*)

Based on the personal values and morals of an individual, they will identify as a member or non-member of an ambiguous crowd.

So why do crowds make things "catch on?" Everyone has been a part of, or at least seen, a "wave" manifest itself at a sporting event and either catch on – or not. Sometimes it takes a few tries by a handful of people before it catches on. Sometimes it takes just once. Sometimes it travels around the stadium multiple times; sometimes, it peters out halfway through. Is it possible there's a science behind this that can explain why certain ideas are embraced by a crowd, and others not?

A wave is defined as a disturbance that travels through a medium. Like water, social media is also a medium, so like a wave in water, ideas make their way through the connected Internet much in the same way. In this case, the ideas are the energy force, and the strength of the idea determines the speed that it travels across channels, and how disruptive it is to its environment around it. Each person in an "idea wave" need only move up and down – in the case of social sharing, that means sharing an idea through a social channel – but when done in concert with many people, a new structure rolls around the "social stadium", best illustrated here by using Brian Solis' "Conversation Prism".

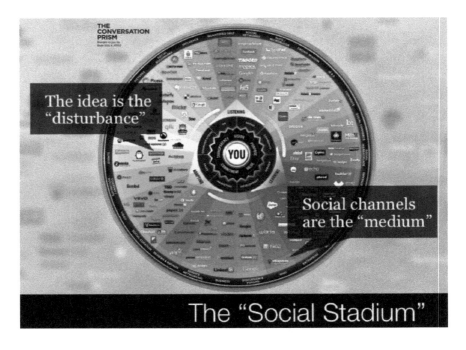

Anyone can start an idea, but what makes people push it through these mediums? Disruption. All it takes is one person to "stand up" in these mediums to make an idea go around the stadium.

Disruption can be delightful. It can also be dark. We've all experienced the dark side of disruption. Like when you're on a website and out of nowhere, an ad takes over the page, unexpectedly covering the content you want to consume. Or that video that auto plays without warning, leaving you scrambling to find the window it's in and diving for your mute button on your keyboard. Even on TV (before DVR!), when we were forced to endure those annoying commercials that turned up the sound 4 times that of the program we were watching.

Dark disruption – it doesn't work, folks. It may get my attention, but the impression it leaves me with is negative, and won't make me buy your stuff.

I prefer the delightful side of disruption. The kind that makes me smile, or shed a tear, connecting with me in a human place that forces me to stop, pay attention, and for a very short time, take me along the journey with it.

Recall a truly magical moment that happened in your life. Our brains do a funny thing when we connect with a magical moment – we create a photographed memory the likes of which lasts a lifetime. These created experiences should be the ultimate goal in business and life.

Delightfully Disruptive Success Story: #SFBatkid

On Friday, Nov. 15, 2013, The Make-A-Wish Foundation Bay Area granted 5-year-old Leukemia survivor Miles Scott his wish of being Batkid for a day. San Francisco officials, SF Chronicle, SF Giants, city businesses and over 11,000 volunteers came together to transform the city into Gotham City. Although it took months of planning, a blogger picked up the story two weeks prior and posted it to Reddit. From there, the story went viral, and almost overnight generated over 70K Likes on Facebook. As the day itself unfolded, USA Today, CNN, Washington Post and other national news reported it in real time on Twitter. Celebrities joined in; Ben Affleck congratulated Batkid for being the "Best Batman Ever", and President Obama made an infamous Vine video letting Miles know that "we're all behind you." Obama's Tweet was retweeted over 8,000 times. I can barely write about it without tearing up, remembering my own experience virtually cheering him on and watching Batkid's wish come true before my, and the world's, eyes. [You can watch a great compilation video online, well done by the Make A Wish Foundation Bay Area.]

So why did this effort, and so many others like it, appeal to the crowd?

The Four "Secrets" to Making Ideas Crowd Worthy:

Secret #1: Use a Universally simple human concept.

Make a boy's wish come true. Delight your customers. Prove a point.

Secret #2 Have a structured plan.

Use a calendar. Get a team behind you. Know your end goal.

Secret #3: Apply the rules of Improv.

There's no "No"; say "yes" to ideas from crowd. The energy of the crowd is contagious and timely. Just go with it.

Secret #4: Invite your people to the party.

Ask them to be a part of it. Keep it real. Make it simple to do and share. Reward and thank them.

Brian Solis said, "Without zeroing in on the root impact of disruption, businesses may be missing tremendous opportunities or, worse, making an investment in what I refer to as digital Darwinism." Do better, or die. It's pretty simple.

Key Takeaway: Brands need to work harder to craft magical moments to create everlasting loyalty to your product or brand. Yes, it's a moving target, but if you're not afraid to embrace emerging social tools and shed your fear of failure, the joy, surprise and delight of your customers will be nothing short of magical.

Chapter 5: Where Do Marketers Go From Here?

When you screw up, just say you're sorry. And mean it.
I think Todd Wilms put this best: *"I think what people are looking for is, how do you own up to a mistake after the fact? If you make a mistake and you apologize sincerely, I think people will forgive that and you move on. I think it's when you come back with older, more traditional PR tactics and say "Gee, this wasn't our problem", I think most people will actually rise up and become quite incensed by it because it sounds like traditional PR gobbledygook. I think most people feel like social is such a human medium that to come in and try and trick your way out of a scenario like that, I think it just backlashes on folks."*

Make an effort to build real relationships. Robert Scoble, technology futurist and Rackspace evangelist said, "I don't see the future, I just have great friends." Relationships are the new currency in today's social world. My friend Ted Rubin also preaches this in his "Return on Relationship" (#RonR) philosophy, which he describes as *the value that is accrued by a person or brand due to nurturing a relationship.* ROR goes beyond ROI, which is just dollars and cents; it's the value (both perceived and real) that will accrue over time through loyalty, recommendations and sharing. One of my favorite Ted Rubin stories is his experience with JetBlue years ago when he was stuck on the tarmac for hours with a plane full of passengers, all of whom desperately wanted to understand what the delay was. The pilots and crew communicated what they could, but it was only Ted's direct communication with the JetBlue social team on Twitter that provided the reason for the delay, since the social team had access to more relevant information than the pilots. Not only did Ted become the plane's "spokesperson", he also successfully procured free movies for everyone on the plane. He later met the man behind the JetBlue social team, on a panel at which they were both speaking. Not only did this man remember the interaction, he also was able to finally thank Ted in-person for helping to elevate the JetBlue brand in a time of crisis, when their brand was at high risk for losing serious future customers, all for bad weather – something completely out of their control. This is a perfect example of how the simplest of interactions in social can ripple into real "RonR".

You don't have to have it all figured out: How about Apple? Steve Wozniak and Steve Jobs originally set out with a simple vision to build a personal computer. They built the first personal computer that delivered a word processor. It turned out that the computer called for the networking, which quickly grew into the need for the Internet. We needed a way to see the new clusters of information created on the Internet, so search engines were born. And now, social commerce is enabled. According to Wozniak, "We did not build a computer knowing all this was going to happen, we started with a simple vision." And despite being a titan of technology, it's refreshing to know that Wozniak is a firm believer that technology will never replace humans. "Brute force doesn't solve anything; it's the methods that come from the human brain that can solve them," said Wozniak. "Human beings need to think through the big ideas in the world."

Keep it simple. Just get to the point. We're all busy. We care about a lot of stuff. Just do less talking and more listening. This applies to messaging, content, conversations – and relationships.

Just be helpful. To reiterate Jay Baer, just be helpful. As people, as a brand, humans see value in this.

Do what you say you'll do. Fulfilling promises builds trust, and if you don't deliver, trust crumbles. It only takes one time to make this happen, and forever to earn it back. Whether it's how you promise to change after a crisis, how you promise to deliver a service or product, or how you promise to act in exchange for an action, it's all the same. Do what you say you'll do. Period.

Become better storytellers. A commonality between humans is our emotions; we can't help crying when others cry, laughing when others laugh. You can't expect anyone to connect with your content, message, brand, values, if you don't yourself. It's that simple. Storytelling is a great way to communicate how you feel, or how you want your audience to feel. A story helps us understand how things fit into our individual experiences and gives us context to make decisions. Stories add the color, personality and relevance about what you're trying to sell. Technology and unsexy products will never go away and need to be sold, but shiny pieces of metal on their own will never be as interesting as the human interpretation of why they exist.

Yes, certain audiences will understand stories about certain products that appeal to them more, but there is a standard of excellence you should be holding your brand to in your campaigns as well; 52% of consumers stop following a business' page because the content is boring and repetitive *(source: SMI)*. So make your marketing interesting. Create a mood through imagery. Speak at your audience's level. Be smart and clever when you can. Tell me, don't sell me.

52% of consumers stop following a business' page because the content is boring and repetitive.

Chapter 6: Being Human Marketers

We often talk at the agency about the difference between balance and harmony. Balance seeks equilibrium and steadiness; harmony seeks agreement and continuity in all of its parts. For marketers, any socially enabled campaign today should be approached with the understanding that there are many elements that are just out of our control. We see social and digital campaigns as a harmonious "Mobius strip", an endless, unbroken chain that perpetuates itself with the right mix of content and context.

To keep this chain constantly moving, this means applying the "Four Rules of Social Context" on our own work. It means we have to work hard to distill the complex into simplicity in what we're communicating. And tap into the "Six Basic Human Needs" to find the connection points we all resonate with. Social and marketing need to work together to personalize individual conversations, as well as deliver shared global experiences from which crowds of common values can benefit. This is what our social and digital mediums have gifted us, and how humans interact and feel more compelled take action.

It's the dichotomy between marketing and social channels that are constantly fighting within themselves to strike a balance in the purpose they serve. It used to be that marketing was a one-to-many medium, broadcasting in broad stroke in the hopes it would be heard. Today, marketing increasingly strives to be one-to-one, with new technologies and solutions popping up every day to collect and wrangle big data about us, and our customers, in an effort to serve up more personalized offers and experiences. On the other hand, social was created as a medium that enabled intimate, one-to-one or one-to a-few online relationships. Today, social has become a more public and vast medium, where the things we share skyrocket quickly to a one-to-many experience.

So in all of this, what can we control as marketers?

Our approach. Our understanding. Our message. We can choose how we want to socially interact with our employees and customers, and control the most important contextual components of our interactions. Knowing this, it's a smarter decision to choose to focus on what is in our control, and what is not. We can choose to try and fail, we can choose to learn from our mistakes, and we can choose to tap into our humanness to connect with others on this level.

Human beings are innately complex yet strive for simplicity. It's the simplicity of our favorite communicators, brands and products that make us fall in love with them, because we get what they're saying. It takes a lot of hard work to make something so complex look so easy. Some call it brilliance, but perhaps we should call it speaking human.

Our challenge as humans is to find, understand and explain the complex in its most simplistic form. Find the commonality in our humanity, and speak the language we've all been waiting for.

That's Human to Human: #H2H.

 Bryan Kramer

About the Author

Bryan is a Social Business Strategist and CEO of PureMatter, where he's led his agency to consistent growth over the last 10 years earning a spot as one of Silicon Valley's fastest growing private companies by the Silicon Valley Business Journal.

Bryan has been listed as the 39th most talked about person on Twitter by global senior marketers in a study via LeadTail, #26 by Kred as a Global Top CEO Influencer on Social Media and as one of The Top 50 Social Global CEOs on Twitter by the Huffington Post. He was also identified as a Top 25 Influencer to follow on Forbes.com. PureMatter is listed as one the Top 50 Twitter accounts to follow by American Express Open.

Being a veracious consumer of knowledge, understanding social media and how it works both as a communication channel and shaper of popular culture has his full attention. With over 150k+ social followers, Bryan has quickly become one of the country's leading authorities on social and digital, speaking in the U.S. and internationally on a variety of topics.

Bryan also hosts "From the Author's Point of View" author podcast series, as well as PureMatter's #Substance Luminary Video Series.

He is a featured contributor on SocialMediaToday.com, Business2Community and the IBM Smarter Commerce blog.

See his full bio at:
http://www.purematter.com/team/bryan-kramer/

Resources

Follow Bryan Kramer in social:

- Blog: www.bryankramer.com

- Twitter: @bryankramer

- Facebook: www.facebook.com/bryankramer

- LinkedIn: www.linkedin.com/in/bryanjkramer

- Google+: /bryankramer

PureMatter #Substance Luminary Video Series:
https://www.youtube.com/user/Purematter

To learn more about PureMatter, visit www.purematter.com

Socially connect with the awesome humans mentioned in this book:

Kare Anderson @KareAnderson

Jay Baer @jaybaer

Johnathan Becher @jbecher

Ellen Degeneres @TheEllenShow

Scott Hebner @SLHebner

Charlene Li @charleneli

Tony Robbins @tonyrobbins

Ted Rubin @TedRubin

Mark Schaefer @markwschaefer

Robert Scoble @Scobleizer

Courtney Smith @cshasarrived

Brian Solis @briansolis

Ben Stiller @RedHourBen

DJ Waldow @djwaldow

Todd Wilms @toddmwilms

Steve Wozniak @stevewoz

Stay in the conversation by adding **#H2H**
to your social content!

Author Q&A

What has changed in business with the advent of social media in just the last few years?

The mass adoption of social media has really put a magnifying glass on business. It used to be that brands could rise by pushing out a one-way conversation to their audience, and that was accepted. But now that social has enabled very global and public conversations, brands are struggling with how to find their voice. There's a lot of fear within businesses because of social that I talk about in the book.

The businesses that have embraced social as a positive channel to engage in conversations with both employees and customers – what we call social business – are really winning. But it takes a lot of training, boundary setting and an open mind. Not many brands have that yet in their leadership.

How has our language changed as we speak to each other online?

Between the convergence of social, mobile and digital technologies, the way we have learned as humans to communicate with each other has changed forever. Texting has enabled us to eliminate face to face, or at least mouth to ear, communications in short bursts. Character limits, like on Twitter, force us to be more succinct about the words we share with the public.

Over 90% of human communication is conveyed through visual body language cues. So what happens, when technology leaves us with just under the remaining 10% of verbal non-visual communication, is a floodgate of communication without context. This is a huge problem that's rewiring our human brains, in my opinion. Humans require context to understand concepts. Without boundaries, short bursts of communication, coupled with a faster-paced, noisy society and shorter attention spans is affecting how we, as humans, tell stories.

Of course, over time, we will adapt to this new form of communication. Maybe it will force people to ask more questions to grasp context before reacting? But for now, I fear that the social/digital/mobile world has created an angry mob of anonymous reactors who take short form communication literally. Until we learn to be mindful of what and how we share – what I call our "social body language" – and exercise our human empathy toward the mistakes and failures of strangers and the people we know, the online world of communication will remain somewhat of the "Wild West."

How does this translate into social and business listening?

As I mention in the book, "listening" is the mother of all senses. What this means in a business context is monitoring social and digital channels for conversations about your brand. "Active listening" goes a step further in reaching out to individuals in social channels to engage them in a public conversation.

There are specific examples in the book about brands who simply weren't listening when a customer shared a picture, or talked negatively about their brand on a social channel, and suffered real monetary consequences like dropped stock prices or loss of customers, because of it. Also to consider is the time and resources it took to try to make it right. I call this a "wrecking ball" for brands, because it can literally do as much damage.

There are brands that are getting it right though. In my own experience, Virgin America gets it. They are actively listening in social, and respond in a timely manner to conversations that make sense for them. On a recent trip to a conference, as I was cruising at 30,000 feet, I tweeted out a response to the conference organizer about how excited I was to be speaking, and mentioned how happy I was flying my favorite airline @VirginAmerica.

Within minutes, their social team responded with an acknowledgment, thanking me for the tweet and wishing me a great time in Orlando. What's remarkable about this is I never mentioned I was flying to Orlando in my tweet. The only information they had from me was the name of the conference – #IBMConnect – and they took it upon themselves to look up where the conference was being hosted, and responded accordingly.

Because Virgin America has empowered their teams to actively listen, this is the perfect example of what I talk about in the book; a "shining moment" opportunity to forge a strong brand impression through listening. And it certainly made an impression on me; not only did I add the example to my presentation at IBM Connect, I am sharing it with you today again.

A lot of people ask me what social listening tools to use. There are so many of them, I say use the one that's right for your brand and workflow. The real question I think they should be asking is "how do I set my employees up for success to help monitor these online conversations?"

No tool can replace a real human interaction, and there are plenty of opportunities in social media to interact. No single community manager could handle it, so why not empower your own biggest fans of your brand to quickly engage?

Humans just want to be heard, and it's our natural tendency to raise our voice when we feel like we're not being heard. If a brand's not listening, social is the loudest megaphone angry customers will ever have.

Notes

There is no B2B and B2C. Human to Human: #H2H